Outsourcing and using a Virtual Assistant for Fun and Profit

By David Holowiski

ISBN 978-0-557-04347-7

Outsourcing and Using a Virtual Assistant for Fun and Profiit
Author: Dave Holowiski

Outsourcing and using a Virtual Assistant for fun and profit

Table of Contents

Outsourcing and Using a Virtual Assistant for Fun and Profiit
Author: Dave Holowiski

What tasks to send to your VA?

How to delegate tasks

A note on impossibly short time frames

Other baby step projects for your VA

7. **Building many relationships and a trusted list: Baby projects**

    Easy 'test' tasks to outsource

    Why two groups?

    A Note on high risk, expensive, or one time projects

    Taking it to the next level

    Tasks you can assign now:

    Lather, Rinse, Repeat, Profit.

8. **Bonus Report: High Volume Low Cost Outsourcing with Amazon Mechanical Turk**

9. **Bonus Report: Outsourcing Order Fulfillment and customer service**

10. **Bonus Report: Payment/escrow/feedback**

Outsourcing and Using a Virtual Assistant for Fun and Profiit
Author: Dave Holowiski

Introduction

"A man is rich in proportion to the number of things he can afford to let alone" – **Henry David Thoreau**

If you are anything like me, your life as an Internet Marketer is overwhelming. It is filled with juggling dozens of different projects, while still trying to enjoy a personal life.

If you are not there yet, you've found this ebook at the right time. If you're there already, take a deep breath and relax, I'm going to help you.

If you follow the easy instructions in this ebook, by the time you finish you will have more time to relax, enjoy life and make gobs of money doing it.

You are about to learn the secrets that Millionaire Internet Marketers and the CEO's of Fortune 500 companies have known for years. Why spend hours everyday writing articles, posting to blogs and doing background research?

You can hire someone who is better, faster and yes even cheaper than you to do the

Outsourcing and Using a Virtual Assistant for Fun and Profiit
Author: Dave Holowiski

grunt work, so you can spend your time coming up with the multi-million dollar ideas and cashing the checks!

Some day you won't even have to cash the checks, you'll have somebody to do it for you! So sit back, read on and see how deep the rabbit hole goes.

Outsourcing and Using a Virtual Assistant for Fun and Profiit
Author: Dave Holowiski

What is outsourcing and why outsource?

"Do not let what you cannot do interfere with what you can do." - **John Wooden**

Chances are you've heard of outsourcing before. You may have even started in Internet Marketing because your job was outsourced overseas and left you unemployed- but if not you've heard in the news of the exodus of information workers from North America and Europe to third and second world countries.

Even so, let's take a minute and examine what outsourcing really is. Outsourcing simply means that somebody is paying a third party to do work that they (or their business) would normally do.

The most well known example is that large Fortune 500 companies are outsourcing their customer service centers to India.

Actually *India* is becoming an expensive country to outsource to as the standard of living is increasing but other countries such as China, Vietnam and Russia / Ukraine / Belorussia are still very inexpensive.

7

Why would you want to outsource your work - either individually or as a business?

For two reasons:
- To save money
- Because you don't have the time or skill to do the work yourself

For businesses it's an easy equation. Employee A costs $50 an hour working in our corporate headquarters, but we can pay somebody in a developing country $10 an hour to do the same job. That means they save $40 an hour for each position you outsource. Over several hundred employees, at 40 hours a week,

the savings quickly runs into the millions of dollars. You can see why outsourcing is so popular!

As for skills, often this is inevitable. Software programmers are so hard to find in some North American cities that companies have to outsource software development simply because they can't hire enough people.

So what about you, as an individual?
Chances are, you are running a business of 1

8

- you! And how much do you get paid an hour? You might be tempted to say nothing, but nothing could be further from the truth.

Let's say that you run a series of blogs and you make money on Adsense from Google. You post 2 articles each to 5 blogs a day. It takes you half an hour to write each article and about an hour to proofread & post to the sites. That's 10 articles a day, which take you about 6 hours in total. That leaves you an extra two hours of time to do research, network and think up new ideas.

Let's say you make $4000 a month on all 5 blogs combined. That works out to $25 an hour, working 8 hours a day, 5 days a week.

But wait - you're working the 9-5, you may as well trade in your pajamas for a suit & tie and head into the office - you'd be making more, with benefits there anyway!

However, you can easily outsource those 10 articles a day for $2-3 each. As a worst case, that's $30 a day for 10 articles. Multiplied over 20 days that's $600. Now subtract that from your monthly income - $4000-$600 = $3400. That's a pay cut of about 15%. That

Outsourcing and Using a Virtual Assistant for Fun and Profiit
Author: Dave Holowiski

may sound high, but now think about what you got for that 15% pay cut.

You are now working 2 hours a day instead of 8! Forget the 9-5, you're working the 11-1! Or even better yet, you could work one 10 hour day a week and take the rest of the week off - imagine taking 6 day weekends every week - what would your mother think?

Take a second and think about this a different way. Suppose you only had another week to live. How much would you pay to spend another hour of life? 5 dollars an hour? 10, 100, 1,000,000? The thought is almost offensive.

But life is short and nobody knows how much time they have left, so we put ridiculous values on an hour of our time (such as $0). Why spend your life working when you can make a little money work for you and give you back the rest of your life?

But you're the typical dedicated, driven, passionate Internet Marketer, chances are you won't be happy working only two hours a day. Sure you'll probably enjoy the first week, especially after years of working 40+ hours a

Outsourcing and Using a Virtual Assistant for Fun and Profiit
Author: Dave Holowiski

week. But before long you'll start to get bored and you'll start to make your business better.

Now imagine, instead of spending 2 hours a day working, if you doubled that and spent four.

- What if you could spend two hours, every day 5 days a week, doing nothing but thinking how you could make more money?

Remember that you're still working only 4 hours a day so you're already incredibly refreshed and focused. Could you increase your profit by 50%?, 100%?, even 200%? This is like compound interest on steroids and the math is simple. You used to make $4000 a month, but now you're only making $3400.

But you work 1/2 as much and have more time to think about growing your profits. So before long you've doubled your profits - now you're making $6800 a month.

That $600 a month wasn't a cost, it was an investment and it's now making you an extra $2800 a month! That's almost a 60% ROI - per month!

Outsourcing and Using a Virtual Assistant for Fun and Profiit
Author: Dave Holowiski

Virtual assistants and outsourcing do not cost money. They make it.

Outsourcing and Using a Virtual Assistant for Fun and Profiit
Author: Dave Holowiski

Virtual Assistants, outsourcing tasks and which country to choose

"Don't be afraid to take a big step when one is indicated. You can't cross a chasm in two small steps"-- **David Loyd George**

First off I'm going to make a distinction here that you may never have thought of or heard anybody else use. There is a difference between getting a Virtual Assistant and outsourcing specific tasks. There are very different qualities you should look for and you will receive the best benefits if you use a good mix of both.

Virtual Assistants

Think of your virtual assistant as your own personal secretary (or administrative assistant if you're the politically correct kind of person). He or she be will a person you want to build a relationship with. They will learn about your company and will learn to anticipate your needs, as you learn their strengths and weaknesses.

13

Think of it as a marriage - sort of. You need to make a dedication to each other and you're both going to have to spend some time getting to know each other. Your virtual assistant will (metaphorically) cook, clean and do the laundry for you, so that you can focus on bringing in the big bucks.

Don't stretch the metaphor too far though - if your virtual assistant isn't working out - divorce their butt - **fire them**. You will go through a few before you find one that really fits (don't worry it's all part of the plan.

What kind of tasks can you source out to your virtual assistant?

- Email - filtering your email, answering customer service questions, flagging email for your attention, filing email in appropriate folders and deleting spam.
- Presentations - no need for you to do the hard work when they can send you a Powerpoint file all ready to go
- Research a new niche, or find out all you can about your biggest competitor.
- Paying affiliates, collecting checks, handling customer refunds etc.

Outsourcing and Using a Virtual Assistant for Fun and Profiit
Author: Dave Holowiski

- Compiling statistics from all of your on-line ventures into a daily/weekly report
- Booking hotel rooms, plane tickets, conference rooms for meetings

These are just a few ideas to get your mind working... you'll think of more by the time you've finished this ebook. Once your VA has gotten to know you, chances are they'll offer to do things for you that you never thought of (if they don't it's time for a new one).

When you are looking for a VA, you will probably notice that many VA's offer to do the types of tasks I recommend outsourcing individually. There is a gray area between the two, but if you think of your VA as a business partner (they aren't though) and your Outsourcers as the 'grunt workers' it will be obvious who should do what work.

Outsourcing individual tasks:

There are many tasks that you will not want to have your VA do. They may not have the skills that are needed, or their hourly rate is too high compared to what you can pay for by the task.

Outsourcing and Using a Virtual Assistant for Fun and Profiit
Author: Dave Holowiski

Remember that you will be paying more per hour for a virtual assistant, because you're expecting to develop a relationship. This is where outsourcing individual tasks (called simply 'outsourcing' for the rest of this ebook) comes into play.

What kind of tasks can you outsource?

- Posting to blogs and social networking sites
- Writing and submitting articles under your name (or a pseudonym)
- Building web sites, writing code, modifying web sites
- Ghost writing an ebook (Yes, many Ebooks are outsourced!)
- Posting to discussion forums and driving traffic to your web sites
- Transcription of audio or video to text (or text to audio or video
- And much more!

Depending on the type of project you are working on, you will find many other tasks that you can outsource. The sky's the limit - you can even outsource product creation entirely to Outsourcers.

Outsourcing and Using a Virtual Assistant for Fun and Profiit
Author: Dave Holowiski

What shouldn't you outsource or assign to a VA?

None!
It will take some time before you reach this comfort level. As we will discuss later, you will slowly build up to the big, important tasks. At first you will outsource the simple tasks until you know the people you have found are reliable and competent.

Eventually you will assign more important sensitive tasks.

The baby steps chapters go into this in detail.

Which Country to choose?
To be honest it is personal preference, but there are essentially two choices.

• Somebody in your own country
• Somebody in a developing or third world country.

If you live in the North America or Europe some of the benefits to outsourcing or getting a Virtual Assistant in your own country are:

Outsourcing and Using a Virtual Assistant for Fun and Profiit
Author: Dave Holowiski

- It's easy to find somebody who speaks your language fluently and understands local slang and sayings.
- Time zones are the same. If you need someone you can call on or email while you are working, this will be important for you. Likewise if you need tasks completed immediately.
- You pay them in the local currency - their hourly rate won't fluctuate from day to day as it could if you were paying them in another currency.

Some of the benefits to getting somebody in a developing country are:

- Much cheaper
- They work while you are in bed - assign them a task before you finish working for the day and it's done when you wake up.
- Because they may be working for several times what the average person makes in their country, they have a vested interest in keeping you happy.

Your major criteria for hiring a Virtual Assistant should be their skills and you will probably find that the country they live in makes little difference (as long as their English skills are OK).

How to find a Virtual Assistant

E pluribus unum. (Out of many, one.) -- **Motto for the seal of the United States.**

Your first step is to have a look at the following web sites and get to know the lingo. You'll want to check out as many options as possible.   Search for the term "Virtual Assistant", "Secretary", or "Assistant".

- www.elance.com
- ivaa.org
- workaholics4hire.com (Internet Marketing oriented)
- getfriday.com (they have been overwhelmed by the recommendation in "The 4-hour work week")
- www.teamdoubleclick.com

What qualifications should you look for?

Set the bar high - some of the qualifications will be faked and remember they're trying to impress you.

Look for or ask for:

Outsourcing and Using a Virtual Assistant for Fun and Profiit
Author: Dave Holowiski

- A college or university degree.
- Somebody who is fluent in English, both written and spoken (even if you don't need it)
- Response times - ask them a question. The answer is not necessarily important, prompt response is
- Look for VA's who are either part of a large outsourcing company overseas) or part of an association (North America) such as AVOA, IVAA or VANA
- Experience, the more the better
- Good feedback from other clients, if the site supports it. Don't consider anybody who is brand new.
- Are they willing to work weekends or late/early hours?

Insider Secret: A seasoned (desirable) North American VA may refuse to work weekends. Newer less experienced VA's will work at any and all times for you, but they won't be as good as a seasoned veteran. This may not apply in other countries.

- Do they have previous experience as a administrative assistant, or executive assistant? If so and if it was more than a year, you've found a winner!

Outsourcing and Using a Virtual Assistant for Fun and Profiit
Author: Dave Holowiski

Do not hire friends or family. There is a fundamental difference when you hire friends or family- No matter how much you trust them, you will have problems. They will not get the work done on time (or at all) because they know you will forgive them, they know you won't get mad at them and you're far less likely to fire them.

How much to pay?

- VA's from developing countries will usually run $4-15 an hour, the lower end being able to handle only simple tasks.
- VA's in North America usually range from $25-$100 an hour.

Don't make a decision solely on cost per hour though. Because of the language barrier, conversing back and forth with somebody in India will eat up hours quickly and a VA in North America is more likely to 'be in tune with you', anticipate your needs, give you "knock your socks off" service and run the business like they owned it service - you'll just have to pay for it.

Insider secret: Once you have found a VA that works well with you, offer to pay them directly via Paypal, rather than through the

Outsourcing and Using a Virtual Assistant for Fun and Profiit
Author: Dave Holowiski

site you found them at. Usually these sites charge some kind of commission and you should be able to negotiate a rate reduction if you pay them directly (this may be against the web site's terms of service - be careful).

Do not do this as you are starting out or for a VA that you've never used before.

The benefit of paying them through the web site is the protection the site offers and the threat of negative feedback, which can ruin a flaky VA's career.

Before you send your VA your their task, make sure there is a contract in place specifying the hourly rate, as well as billing increments (will they bill you in 15 minute, 1/2 hour, 1 hour portions?)

You're going to need to sample several before you find one that really 'clicks' and it's better to start off at the cheap end while you're learning.

Outsourcing and Using a Virtual Assistant for Fun and Profiit
Author: Dave Holowiski

Where to find an Outsourcer

"Every organization must be prepared to abandon everything it does to survive in the future" -- **Peter Drucker**

Note: Country is mostly irrelevant here. Pick the most qualified person for the best price. Specify fluency in English only if necessary (it often isn't).

First you are going to want to define the tasks you want to outsource. Start simple and build up to more complex tasks.

Web sites to look at:

www.rentacoder.com
- programming (HTML, software, web apps)
- graphic design
- marketing/advertising
- writing/translation

The following link has a complete list of categories:
http://www.rentacoder.com/RentACoder/Softw areCoders/BrowseWork.asp

www.elance.com
• everything you could ever imagine and more

Note: Elance is the most 'mainstream' of the outsourcing sites. This can mean higher prices and more scams. Be careful.

www.articleauthors.net
• articles
• ebooks
• copyediting
• press releases
• ghost writing

Prices are fixed and you are not dealing with an individual - later on we will focus on building relationships which is difficult to do at such a site.

www.guru.com
• web site design/marketing
• graphic design (all kinds)
• marketing
• writing/editing/translating
• programming

This site includes categories for quite a few more 'traditional' business functions as well, such as engineering, telephone systems, accounting etc.

www.odesk.com
- web development and programming
- audio and video production including voice talent
- software development
- writing of all kinds
- graphics art design
- administrative support

www.youroutsourceteam.com
- SEO (Search Engine Optimization
- PPC advertising
- web design
- content creation

This site is very focused on Internet Marketing

www.craigslist.com
- Anything you can imagine.

This site is basically a huge classified ad

Last but certainly not least, try your local university or college. There are thousands of well educated starving students there looking to make a quick buck.

The quality is definitely hit or miss, but I've found some of my best Outsourcers here.

25

Building a relationship: Baby steps: Virtual Assistant

"Never tell people how to do things. Tell them what to do and they will surprise you with their ingenuity." **--General George Smith Patton, Jr.**

Building a relationship with your virtual assistant is important. When you find a virtual assistant that works well for you, you will want to keep them for as long as you can and pay them well.

Be prepared to try several different virtual assistants out when you are starting, it will take some time before you find one that understands your needs and works well for you.

Virtual Assistants vary widely in the types of services they provide.

Sometimes what your virtual assistant will do and what your an Outsourcer do will overlap. If you're trying to figure out what task you

Outsourcing and Using a Virtual Assistant for Fun and Profiit
Author: Dave Holowiski

should assign to one or the other, keep this rule of thumb in mind:

In general your virtual assistant will provide higher quality work, but cost more. An Outsourcer will probably do the job faster and for less money, but the quality will be much less.

What tasks to send to your VA?

It is important that you start a new VA with non mission-critical tasks, designed to test their quality and skill as a Virtual Assistant.

An excellent first task is research. Let's say you want to find out about a competitor of yours, or you need to get some information for a product you're thinking of selling. This is an excellent first task for your VA because you're going to test their skill at finding and summarizing information and you'll also be testing their English skills (important if English is not their native language).

But don't just tell them "Find out all you can about product X" or you may have a nasty surprise, because you have left this task wide open to interpretation. Since you're paying them by the hour, they could spend the next

27

40 hours doing research and come back with 100 pages of text- both extremely expensive and probably too much information for you anyway.

How to delegate tasks

Here's an example of how to ask a VA to do research:

Hello Jane. For your first task, I would like you to research product X (web link here). I am looking for the following information:
- Where available, sales figures: volume and dollar amount, for the last six months
- product reviews - both good and bad (please limit to no more than 10 each). Please summarize the major benefits and drawbacks of this product
- Please provide a list of the top 5 resellers of this product including links to their web sites, as well as a summary of any negative or positive feedback they have received
- Does the author sell Private Label Rights (PLR)? If so please find the price and the details.
- Does the author have an affiliate program? If so please provide selling price, conversion rate and any applicable rules

28

Do not spend more than 2 hours completing this research. If you are not finished after 2 hours, please email me the results in a word file and I will advise you how to proceed.

I need this completed by the end of the day Friday

Please email me back to confirm that you have received this. If you have any questions or need any points clarified, please let me know.

Note the important points here:

- You set a maximum time: 2 hours and said what to do once the time is up
- You asked to confirm receipt of the task. That way it won't 'fall through the cracks' and you won't be scrambling to do the task yourself last minute
- You have outlined the exact information you need - price, reviews, sellers etc. In the cases where there may be too much information, you have limited it (no more than 10 good or bad product reviews) and asked for a summary instead.
- You provided a deadline. You will have this information no later than the end of the day Friday. If they are in another country, don't

29

forget to specific who's Friday - yours or theirs?

- The time frame is quite short. This gives you an idea of how fast your VA works – chances are they won't complete it, so you'll get to see how far they progressed
- For a new VA, set your deadlines well before the actual deadline. In this case if your deadline is Sunday, set their deadline for Friday. You're going to need to double check their work and there is a chance they'll miss the deadline. Even if they're a day late, you are still able to meet the real deadline.

If all goes well you're going to want to send your VA another task fairly soon.

The next task I recommend sending them is fact/grammar checking and correction. In the next chapter you will be getting an Outsourcer to write articles for you – these won't be perfect, so you can give them to your VA to check and correct.

Here is an example of this request:

Hello Jane. Please download the file at the following link: (link here)

Included are 50 articles.

Outsourcing and Using a Virtual Assistant for Fun and Profiit
Author: Dave Holowiski

Please do the following:
- Review each article and correct any grammar or spelling errors.
- Here is a link to the product I am selling: (link here). Please rate the articles on a scale from 1 to 5 with 1 being poor and 5 being excellent, on how well the article does at promoting the product.
- Please send me an email with the edited articles as well as the ratings.

Do not spend more than 1 hour on this project. If you have not completed, please stop and email me the results.

I need this completed by the end of the day Friday

Please email me back to confirm that you have received this. If you have any questions or need any points clarified, please let me know.

I won't go over everything again, but note you've told her exactly what you want, when you want it and how long it should take (again note the impossibly short time frame).

Outsourcing and Using a Virtual Assistant for Fun and Profiit
Author: Dave Holowiski

A note on impossibly short time frames

The reason I start out with impossibly short time frames is to gage how fast the VA is able to work. The first tasks will be returned partially completed, or completed but poor quality.

This is important as you will find out how fast your VA works and how well they work under pressure. Don't feel offended if they come back and flat out tell you you're setting unrealistic deadlines. This is a good thing – a VA who knows how fast they can work and isn't afraid to tell you is one you're going to want to hold on to!

Other baby step projects for your VA

- Provide a project description and ask your VA to collect and rank a list of qualified Outsourcers from a pre-approved list of outsourcing web sites
- Make appointments for you. If you have no business related appointments, have some fun. Have your VA call your friend and schedule dinner, have them book a haircut for you (assuming you've chosen a VA that

32

handles personal tasks as well - some only handle business).
- Research a new niche and compile keywords related to that niche
- Research, research and more research!

Just be careful – you want to challenge your VA but don't give them any tasks that are mission critical, you hardly know them!

At this point it is extremely important to set time limits and firm deadlines to decrease the potential risk. Once you get to know your VA better you might be more flexible with these, because you trust them to use their judgment - this will come with time, approach slowly and carefully.

After you've sent your Virtual Assistant several tasks, have a look over the results.

- If they provided this to you as samples of their previous work, would you
hire them?
- Did they meet their deadlines?
- Did they stay within the maximum time limits?
- Did they finish faster than you expected?

Outsourcing and Using a Virtual Assistant for Fun and Profiit
Author: Dave Holowiski

- Were they able to understand an execute your requests without too much explanation?

This is also a good time to judge the value of the work they've done for you. Make a list of all the tasks they've done for you, how much each one cost in total and how long it would have taken you to do it. This should give you a good idea of the relative value of the work they have done.

Remember that the more of a relationship you build with a VA the more 'bang for the buck' you'll get. Right now they may only be booking haircuts and dinner dates, but some day you'll have them (or a team of them) managing your Outsourcers, answering your email and practically running your business for you.

- If this is your first VA, take a break from them for a week or two (tell them you're going on vacation) and try at least two more, different VA's with similar tasks and pass judgment on them too. Your first VA may be good, but your second or third may unbelievably excellent.

Once you've been through three or more VA's make a decision - keep them or fire them.

Outsourcing and Using a Virtual Assistant for Fun and Profiit
Author: Dave Holowiski

You'll have to fire at least two of them and it's essential you get **used to this now.** Be nice, just tell them that you no longer require their services.

At this point you should have a VA who you know is competent and reliable. Keep your mind open and realize that as time passes you may have to replace them or hire another one – make sure to come back to this chapter and run through the basics again with any new VA.

Outsourcing and Using a Virtual Assistant for Fun and Profiit
Author: Dave Holowiski

Building many relationships and a trusted list: Baby projects

"Good, fast, cheap. Choose any two"
(unknown)

With Outsourcers, this could not be more true. In general you're probably looking for fast and cheap. You can use your VA to add the 'good' (by fixing articles, proofreading etc) later if necessary.

- As you begin to outsource individual tasks, make a list of trustworthy, dependable people, along with the skills they seem to excel in
- Try many different people from many different sites - some will fail you and some will walk away with your money (escrow and starting with small projects is important)

Your trusted list of Outsourcers will become something you can go to when you need something done RIGHT and NOW and you can't take any chances. You can also use this list to find sources for your bigger projects.

Outsourcing and Using a Virtual Assistant for Fun and Profiit
Author: Dave Holowiski

It is important that you make a list of tasks that you want to outsource, for every project.

For example, if you are building a new web site, you would want to list every task that needs to be performed and the time you estimate it will take. Then you want to go through the list and highlight everything that can be outsourced - this should be almost everything.

Until you've found Outsourcers you know you can rely on, split up a task (such as building a web site) in to many much smaller tasks, rather than leaving it as one big (risky) task.

Easy 'test' tasks to outsource

- Writing articles
- Posting to your blog (either as you, them, or under a pseudonym)
- Recording text to Audio (make sure you hear samples first)
- Transcribing audio to text
- Building a 1-2 page web site

At this point, avoid outsourcing tasks where anything is sent directly to your customers or

Outsourcing and Using a Virtual Assistant for Fun and Profiit
Author: Dave Holowiski

to the public without you reviewing it and anything expensive (more than $50-$100).

For example it would be a bad idea to have an Outsourcer that you've never used before posting to discussion forums under your name. If they post to your blog, configure it up so their posts are hidden until YOU approve them.

Remember, they are speaking for you.

• For anything requiring ID's, have them set up their own, rather than using yours. This will save you from having to change your passwords each time you change Outsourcers.

Make sure to use several Outsourcers and it sometimes is a good idea to split a task between several Outsourcers. If you need 100 articles written, have two write 50. This decreases the risk of them not being completed and lets you try out two different Outsourcers (it will cost a little more money but that's ok for now).

You will want to outsource as many tasks as you can, to as many different Outsourcers as possible. Try several different web sites too,

Outsourcing and Using a Virtual Assistant for Fun and Profiit
Author: Dave Holowiski

you'll find there are different types of people on them and people with different skill sets.

The idea here is to sample many Outsourcers with low cost, low risk projects. As with your trial VA, make sure to set aggressive deadlines and make sure they are well before the actual deadline.

Now make a list, as you did with your VA's. There should be many more Outsourcers here though - the exact number depends on how busy you are and how many outsourceable low cost low risk tasks you have.

I recommend tracking this in an excel spreadsheet. Mark off any that did not complete the project, did not meet the deadline, or provided poor quality results. Don't delete their information - you want to keep it so you can know to avoid them. With the rest, categorize them into two groups: provided OK results, or provided Excellent results. Keep track of how much the task cost and don't forget to collect names and email addresses (some outsourcing web sites discourage this but it is vital to our plan).

Why two groups?

Outsourcing and Using a Virtual Assistant for Fun and Profiit
Author: Dave Holowiski

Why keep track of Outsourcers who only do 'OK' results?

In that group of just OK Outsourcers, you'll probably find some very inexpensive ones – higher quality Outsourcers are more likely to be more expensive.

The OK Outsourcers can be your 'go to', high volume Outsourcers. Say you need 200 articles written, or a hundred blog posts. You're probably better off spending less on an OK low cost Outsourcer - and either correcting the results yourself, or better yet having your VA do it.

In the second group you will have the people that provided excellent results. This is the group you go to when money is no object, you need quality and you need it now! This is the group that you eventually want to have posting to forums or you, writing sales copy, sending emails to your customers, building your web site and writing software for you. You will want to have them do progressively more important tasks as you build a higher level of trust and understand their skills.

• Cultivate your excellent, trusted group of Outsourcers. Keep them happy, pay them a

Outsourcing and Using a Virtual Assistant for Fun and Profiit
Author: Dave Holowiski

little more than they ask and give them a bonus every once in a while. If you're there for them (cash wise) they'll be there for you when you have crazy deadlines, near perfect quality demands and high risk projects for them.

This is not a one time process. With each new project you do, make a list of the easy baby step tasks and outsource them to a new group of people. Outsourcers come and go, so you'll constantly need to be refreshing your OK and Trusted lists.

A Note on high risk, expensive, or one time projects

At some point you will need to outsource a large project. This might be building a large complicated web site (such as a subscription membership site), writing a software application, writing an ebook (don't overlook your VA for this one though), or something else.

This is where your trusted Outsourcer list becomes extremely valuable. Look it over and see if you have anybody who already has the skills you need. If not you're going to have to outsource to someone new.

Outsourcing and Using a Virtual Assistant for Fun and Profiit
Author: Dave Holowiski

Check the outsourcing web sites and make sure that you see examples of past similar projects for any prospects. If they are writing software for you, look or ask for other software they have written. If there's a trial version try it out, otherwise buy a copy (or ask them for an evaluation copy). Likewise if it's an ebook - check it out. If possible contact the author and ask them what they thought of the Outsourcer. If it's a web site spend some time there.

Make sure the project closely fits the Outsourcer's skill set. If the site supports it, read their feedback and take it into account. Don't pay them until they are finished and, if it's an expensive project pay them through the site you found them on, even if you've used them many times before. Most sites offer escrow or some kind of arbitration system, so you can be sure you get what you've paid for.

Building relationships: Power tip

If you have found a VA or Outsourcer who is doing exceptional work for you, consider doing a Joint Venture (JV) with them. Rather than paying them to create or market a product for you, make them a partner and split the profits

Outsourcing and Using a Virtual Assistant for Fun and Profiit
Author: Dave Holowiski

with them. Nothing builds loyalty faster than gobs of money!

Taking it to the next level

"The best executive is the one who has sense enough to pick good men to do what he wants done and self-restraint enough to keep from meddling with them while they do it." -- **Theodore Roosevelt**

Now you've laid the groundwork for success. You have one or two good VA's who you know are reliable and skilled and you have a list of good Outsourcers: both OK and cheap and not so cheap but skilled, trusted and excellent.

This is where your outsourcing goes into hyperdrive, your workload decreases exponentially and your profits skyrocket.

As you outsource more and more, you'll build up your team. Eventually you'll have to get a second or third VA. You may even want to consider totally outsourcing order fulfillment and/or customer service.

The following is a template of types of tasks to assign to your Outsourcers. This list slowly

Outsourcing and Using a Virtual Assistant for Fun and Profiit
Author: Dave Holowiski

escalates the level of trust between you and your partners.

Note: VA=Virtual Assistant, OS=Outsourcer

VA: Provide your VA with a task description and budget and have them seek out and qualify Outsourcers. Make sure you have final approval.

OS: Blog posts not in your name, but with the signature pointing to your web site (ask for urls to each post so you (or your VA!) can verify they are working)

VA: Contacting other people within your niche and arranging interviews, exchanging information, networking and discussing joint ventures

OS: Small programming/script work such as integrating your web site with an auto responder, programming pop-ups/pop-unders and exit pages

VA: reviewing and submitting articles for you (provided direct from your Outsourcers to your VA)

OS: Writing sales copy, squeeze pages

Outsourcing and Using a Virtual Assistant for Fun and Profiit
Author: Dave Holowiski

VA: Give access to a shared mailbox, responding to routine customer inquiries

OS: Build larger software applications. Write entire web site. Integrate shopping cart into your site

VA: Note: Somewhere around this point, it is a good idea to have a heart to heart talk with your VA. They are starting to get an understanding of your business. Ask them what other skills they can offer, or what they think they can do to increase the profitability of your business.

Your VA may start to back off a bit here - if they are in it just for the hourly work they may not want to get deeper involved in your business. If they've made it this far, you probably want to keep using them, but it's a good time to think about adding another VA and developing them too.

Approach this carefully, but if they don't back off you may want to consider offering them a commission on sales and enlisting them to much more actively promote your products. They will start to become more of a partner than an assistant.

Outsourcing and Using a Virtual Assistant for Fun and Profiit
Author: Dave Holowiski

OS: Note - this is where your Outsourcers will start to level off. By now you'll have ones that you have tried and tested on large projects and have absolute trust in. You'll also have a large number of Outsourcers to send the day to day drudgery to. Just make sure to constantly keep adding new Outsourcers to balance out the natural attrition rate.

Above this level you'll almost exclusively be relying on your team of VA's. This will partially rely on them having experience with Internet marketing (or they'll be learning from you). This is where your team comes in - some will be willing to get much more involved and some will want to keep it to traditional 'administrative assistant' type tasks. This is fine because you're paying them by the hour - build up a team that has the skills you need and use them 'on demand' as you need them.

Tasks you can assign now:

- Research and identify new niches, new product opportunities
- Handle 100% of customer service inquires
- Compose and send email newsletters to your customers/prospects

Outsourcing and Using a Virtual Assistant for Fun and Profiit
Author: Dave Holowiski

- Seek additional and other types of PR (interviews, radio/news) to build your expert status
- Managing your Outsourcers completely (posting projects, accepting bids, monitoring progress)
- Pay suppliers, collect and cash checks

Outsourcers:
- Build entire products for you - ebooks, audio, physical products (VA to manage)

You see at this point, you literally are just the 'idea man'. Your team of VA's are managing the projects for you, assigning tasks both large and small to Outsourcers and even cashing the checks! All you have to do is lay on the beach, sipping martinis and dreaming up new products.

Lather, Rinse, Repeat, Profit.

You have reached IM nirvana. You have an idea, your VA's are the motivating force and your Outsourcers make it happen.

Welcome to the good life.

Outsourcing and Using a Virtual Assistant for Fun and Profiit
Author: Dave Holowiski

*Whatever the mind can conceive and believe, the mind can achieve."
-- Dr Napoleon Hill*

Bonus Report: High Volume Low Cost Outsourcing with Amazon Mechanical Turk

Amazon Mechanical Turk (www.mturk.com) is kind of a strange outsourcing site. The idea of the site is that thousands of people participate and will do small jobs for you, for small amounts of money.   I've found that this site is best if you need lots of very, very simple tasks performed - if you need something done that requires a human brain (that can't easily be done by computer) you can outsource it here.

Log in and have a look around, what you'll see is many HIT's (Human Intelligence Task) pay about $0.01 to $0.02. Many of the most common tasks are verifying and collecting information. Each request has a certain number of HIT's available – often tens, hundreds or even thousands. This simply means that the task can be performed x number of times (usually with slightly different data).

Outsourcing and Using a Virtual Assistant for Fun and Profiit
Author: Dave Holowiski

Here is a description of a typical request: "You will be determining if two items are exactly the same, or different". Pays $0.01, 10 HIT's available. What this means is that when someone accepts the task, they will be shown two items and have to answer whether they are different or the same. Doing this once will earn $0.01. This request will be available until all of the HIT's have been submitted.

Another common request is transcribing audio - the going rate is about $3 per 10 minutes. The highest paying HIT (aka project) on the site right now pays $10.

How much does it cost? The fee is the number of assignments, multiplied by 10% of the reward, or by the minimum fee of $.005 (yes, half a cent) whichever is greater.

When you are submitting a HIT they have a great calculator that figures it all out for you. Once you've finished browsing requests, make sure to go to the site specifically for creating HIT's: requester.mturk.com

As an example, I was running a hiking blog 2 years ago. It was a brand new site and I needed some content for it, but I didn't have

50

time to write it. The idea of the site was that hikers would blog about hikes they've been on and network with each other.

So I submitted the following HIT request:

"write a hiking article for a small but growing web site"

Please write a hiking article, of at least 200 words. This will appear as a post on a small but growing web site, targeted towards a hiking community. NO PLAGARISM I will verify that it is an original article before approving. If you cite other resources please include URL's. Don't worry too much about the formatting or the spelling, but please be careful with grammar & make sure it is understandable. I am looking for _quality_ writing here, if you submit junk I will reject it.

Article Ideas:

Review a hiking trail (Please include latitude/longditude or a link to a google map)

Review Hiking Equipment

Tell a funny or entertaining (true) hiking story

Outsourcing and Using a Virtual Assistant for Fun and Profiit
Author: Dave Holowiski

Talk about the history of hiking or a newsworthy event

Or anything else you can think of...

Notice I am still being quite specific, although the cost of failure isn't disastrous, as you'll see. I paid $0.50 per article and requested 20. Total cost to me: $10.05. I set the cost per article pretty high - I could have probably spent $0.10 per article, but I did want good grammar (I didn't want to have to fix much).

The results I got back were great and nothing unusable- although even if 1/2 of the results were unusable it still would have been worth it.

Have fun too. I posted another HIT for $0.02 and requested 80.

"Your romantic $.02"

I am a very shy computer geek. There is a girl in the office who I know likes me but I have only ever spoken a few words to her. The only time I see her is passing her in the hallway, or leaving for the day (we leave at the same time). I need your suggestions/schemes/help. Basically, how do I talk to her, what do I say in

Outsourcing and Using a Virtual Assistant for Fun and Profiit
Author: Dave Holowiski

our passing moments? (I've tried "Hi" but it makes for a very short conversation)

Some of the answers I got back were amazing!

On a more practical note, here are some things you can use Mechanical turk for:

- blog postings
- forum posts
- research (works best if there are a lot of similar tasks that can be passed out) - examples I have seen are "find the phone number of pubs in city x"
- •act checking
- transcription (best if you split it up into 10 minute chunks)

Always request more than you need - you're working on volume here and you won't be able to use some of the responses.

Last tip: This is your chance to break all the rules! You are not trying to build a relationship with these people, you will probably never even know their first name.

There is no escrow and no feedback. There is no arbitration system. Your only protection is

Outsourcing and Using a Virtual Assistant for Fun and Profiit
Author: Dave Holowiski

low prices (if you are stiffed for $0.01 the world isn't going to end)

A word on the name: Mechanical Turk

From the mturk.com FAQ:

In 1769, Hungarian nobleman Wolfgang von Kempelen astonished Europe by building a mechanical chess-playing automaton that defeated nearly every opponent it faced. A life-sized wooden mannequin, adorned with a fur-trimmed robe and a turban, Kempelen's "Turk" was seated behind a cabinet and toured Europe confounding such brilliant challengers as Benjamin Franklin and Napoleon Bonaparte. To persuade skeptical audiences, Kempelen would slide open the cabinet's doors to reveal the intricate set of gears, cogs and springs that powered his invention. He convinced them that he had built a machine that made decisions using artificial intelligence. What they did not know was the secret behind the Mechanical Turk: a human chess master cleverly concealed inside.

Today, we build complex software applications based on the things computers do well, such as storing and retrieving large amounts of information or rapidly performing calculations. However, humans still significantly outperform the most powerful computers at completing such simple tasks as identifying objects in photographs—something children can do even before they learn to speak.

When we think of interfaces between human beings and computers, we usually assume that the human being is the one requesting that a task be completed and the computer is completing the task and providing the results. What if this process were reversed and a computer program could ask a human being to perform a task and return the results? What if it could coordinate many human beings to perform a task?

Amazon Mechanical Turk provides a web services API for computers to integrate "artificial artificial intelligence" directly into their processing by making requests of humans. Developers use the Amazon Mechanical Turk web service to submit tasks to the Amazon Mechanical Turk web site, approve completed tasks and incorporate the answers into their software applications. To the application, the transaction looks very much like any remote procedure call: the application sends the request and the service returns the results. Behind the scenes, a network of humans fuels this artificial artificial intelligence by coming to the web site, searching for and completing tasks and receiving payment for their work.

Outsourcing and Using a Virtual Assistant for Fun and Profiit
Author: Dave Holowiski

Bonus Report: Outsourcing Order Fulfillment and customer service

One of the biggest time sinks for an Internet marketer is customer service.

Additionally if you have any kind of a physical product, then order fulfillment follows a close second.

Customer service is something that you can fairly easily outsource to a VA, but it will consume allot of their time and need allot of training. If you do ship a physical product, at a certain point it will be a good idea to hire an end to end fulfillment company who will handle fulfillment and a call center to handle your customers. This leaves you and your team of VA's and Outsourcers to create, market and run the business.

I recommend that once you reach about 20 units shipped a week that you switch over to an end to end fulfilment company.

A few fulfilment companies are:

Outsourcing and Using a Virtual Assistant for Fun and Profiit
Author: Dave Holowiski

Motivational Fulfilment www.mfpsinc.com
Moulton Fulfilment
www.moultonfulfillment.com
National Fulfilment
www.nationalfulfillment.com

A few Customer Service companies:

Global Sky www.global-sky.com
West Teleservices www.west.com
Hero Desk www.herodesk.com
Convergys www.convergys.com
LiveOps www.liveops.com

If you are going to outsource your customer
service, it is extremely important that you have
very well documented procedures.

As you start up your business, keep a folder
that has common questions and complaints
that you get from your customers – along with
the responses. When you outsource your
customer service, you can provide these to
the outsourcing company as canned
responses.

Outsourcing and Using a Virtual Assistant for Fun and Profiit
Author: Dave Holowiski

Bonus Report: Payment/escrow/feedback

As you utilize Virtual Assistants and Outsourcers, you will need to pay them - this is a fact of life and if you figure out how get around this you are a far wiser person than I. It's best you get to know the payment methods.

First, never, ever give an Outsourcer your credit card number. For a VA, wait a long time, if ever before you give them your credit card number. For both Outsourcers and VA's, you will probably start out paying them through the web site you found them on. VA's you will usually pay by the hour, Outsourcers by the task.

For a VA, find out how they prefer to be paid. Count on having to pay them weekly, although some will prefer bi-weekly or monthly. You will make the transition from paying them through a web site to paying them directly via Paypal fairly quickly - once you feel they are trustworthy and you no longer need the

Outsourcing and Using a Virtual Assistant for Fun and Profiit
Author: Dave Holowiski

protection that a web site may provide (through arbitration and negative feedback).

For an Outsourcer, because they are much more transitory and task based, you're going to want to pay them through the site for much longer. Never pay an Outsourcer before the job is done - if they demand it, go elsewhere, you don't want to work with them. If you do ever give an advance, only pay a small percentage of the total fee ahead of time and then only if you trust the Outsourcer.

Before you accept a bid, make sure you understand the protection mechanisms available at the web site. Many offer escrow: this means that at the beginning of the project, you pay the full amount to a third party (often the web site). Once the project is completed to your satisfaction, you release the funds to the Outsourcer.

This gives the Outsourcer some protection - they know that as the money is already there provided they complete the project. This also gives you protection - they don't get the money until you are satisfied the project is complete. If they vanish, the money goes back to you..

Outsourcing and Using a Virtual Assistant for Fun and Profiit
Author: Dave Holowiski

Feedback: On some sites, feedback is your only recourse (ebay is a prime example of this). Before accepting a bid, very carefully scrutinize the Outsourcers feedback for any negative feedback and consider not using anyone who has any negative feedback. If you accept a bid and the Outsourcer doesn't complete the project or doesn't complete it to your satisfaction, you may, or may not have to pay them - read the site rules ahead of time.

The best sites use both feedback and escrow and have some kind of human-based arbitration system. This way feedback does not become something that will ruin your (or an Outsourcer's) reputation and it's easier to take chances on unknowns or people with some negative feedback, knowing you won't have to pay if they don't deliver the goods.

As you develop a relationship with your Outsourcers you will develop trust as well. Once you reach a certain point you will likely feel comfortable paying them directly. This still doesn't mean giving them your credit card number - use Paypal, but it does mean bypassing the web site you found them on. These sites always take some kind of commission, so paying them directly means

Outsourcing and Using a Virtual Assistant for Fun and Profiit
Author: Dave Holowiski

they earn more money. You can also use this as leverage to negotiate a lower price.

However, even with a trusted Outsourcer, if you are doing a large, expensive project, which could seriously harm you financially if they ran away with your money, go back to a web site with an escrow service. You might have to pay a little more, but when that trusted Outsourcer flakes off in the middle of the biggest project of your life, where would you rather have your money - in their bank account, or back in escrow at the web site (where you can recover it)?

One last note on payments: You will almost exclusively be using a credit card to pay Outsourcers and VA's. Make sure to get one and build up your credit limit. It also pays to get one that gives some kind of points - such as air miles or cash back, since you'll be using it heavily you might as well get something back for it.

Outsourcing and Using a Virtual Assistant for Fun and Profiit
Author: Dave Holowiski

Outsourcing and Using a Virtual Assistant for Fun and Profiit
Author: Dave Holowiski

Printed in Great Britain by
Amazon.co.uk, Ltd.,
Marston Gate.